# Do Curve Balls Really Curve?

## by David Fischer

AN AVON CAMELOT BOOK

AVON BOOKS, INC.
1350 Avenue of the Americas
New York, New York 10019

Copyright © 1999 by Creative Media Applications, Inc.
Published by arrangement with Creative Media Applications, Inc.
A Creative Media Applications Production
Art Direction by Fabia Wargin Design
Library of Congress Catalog Card Number: 98-93660
ISBN: 0-380-80362-3
**www.avonbooks.com**

First Avon Camelot Printing: April 1999

CAMELOT TRADEMARK REG. U.S. PAT. OFF. AND IN OTHER COUNTRIES, MARCA REGISTRADA, HECHO EN U.S.A.

Printed in the U.S.A.

OPM 10 9 8 7 6 5 4 3 2

# Introduction

**D**id you know that the high five was started by a volleyball team? Or that the skateboard was invented by frustrated surfers? Or that the Super Bowl got its name from a child's toy?

**Do Curveballs Really Curve?** answers 60 of the most fascinating sports trivia questions you never thought to ask! Find out the stories behind some of the most amazing events in sports. Read about some of the greatest games, most famous legends, and most exciting plays of all time!

This book is a sports fan's ultimate resource. Use it to look up unknown facts, or read it just for fun! Start at the beginning and read straight through to the end, or jump around to find facts about a favorite sport. The book is jam-packed with history on 19 different sports. No matter where you start, one thing is for sure: This book will teach you something about sports you never knew before!

# Do Curveballs Really Curve?

In 1941, **Life** magazine published a strobe-lit photograph of a curveball in motion. This was supposed to prove that the ball doesn't curve—that it is in fact an optical illusion. This fueled the curveball controversy, which didn't let up even after **Life** corrected its error in 1953.

Thanks to a recent book, **The Physics of Baseball,** by Robert K. Adair (a Yale physics professor), we now have undeniable proof that a curveball does curve on both the horizontal and vertical planes. Hitters always knew this, of course; it was journalists who evidently did not.

On the vertical plane the ball curves downward because of topspin (which produces greater air pressure above the ball than below it) and the effect of gravity. On the horizontal plane, the ball also curves away from the side of the higher air pressure as it spins on its axis like a top.

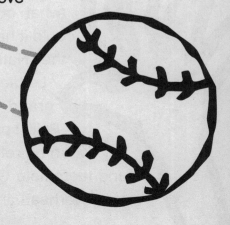

Any pitcher will tell you that the break on his curveball depends on the speed of the pitch and the amount of spin he puts on it. Most pitchers don't know that it also depends on the density of the air. For a more detailed explanation of this subject, we suggest you enroll in Professor Adair's class.

## Who Started the High Five?

The high five became popular when a national audience saw it performed by the Los Angeles Dodgers. The Dodgers may have raised the first high five in baseball, but they don't deserve credit for starting the gesture.

The first Dodger high five occurred in 1977, on October 5 (what other day of the month could it have been?) in Game 2 of the National League playoffs. Leftfielder Dusty Baker hit a grand slam home run off Phillie pitcher Jim Lonborg, and when he returned to the dugout he and teammate Glenn Burke raised their arms overhead and slapped hands.

"That was it—the first [baseball] high five," recalls Dusty, now the manager of the San Francisco Giants. "But I didn't originate it."

The first high five probably occurred during a volleyball game played on a California beach. In fact, Kathy Gregory, women's volleyball coach at the University of California at Santa Barbara, recalls that high fives and high tens first became common in her sport as early as the late 1960s, perhaps because players were used to reaching high and hitting hands above the net.

"If a girl hit a ball out or made some other mistake, we just went up and high-slapped her," says Coach Gregory. "You know, women give so much more support to each other than men do... For every one high five they did, we must have high-fived a million times."

## Why Do Umpires Use Hand Signals?

Dummy Hoy was the first deaf baseball player. The 5'4" Hoy played the outfield for six teams from 1888 to 1902 and had a lifetime average of .288. That was not good enough to get him to the Hall of Fame, but he did leave his mark in another way. Because of his hearing impairment, umpires began to use hand signals to call balls and strikes.

Another deaf player of that era was Dummy Taylor, who pitched for John McGraw's New York Giants from 1900 to 1908. Runners had trouble stealing when he pitched, and sportswriters of the day claimed Taylor could read the faces of would-be base stealers. A current deaf baseball player is Atlanta Braves outfielder Curtis Pride. Pride is the fifth deaf man to play major league baseball.

There have been a number of hearing-impaired athletes in other sports, most notably football. Larry Brown, the former Pro Bowl running back for the Redskins, was born deaf in his right ear and played with a hearing aid in his helmet. Bonnie Ryan Sloane, who played four games as defensive tackle for the St. Louis Cardinals in 1973, was the first totally deaf NFL player. The second was Kenny Walker, who played linebacker for the Denver Broncos in 1991 and 1992.

# Who Started the Slam-Dunk?

**B**ob Kurland, a 6'10" center for Oklahoma A&M, was the first to regularly make use of the slam-dunk—it wasn't yet known by that name—and in 1945 the new weapon proved unstoppable as the Aggies won the NCAA championship. The following season Kurland led the nation in scoring, and A&M became the first school ever to win two straight NCAA titles. Kurland was the tournament MVP both times.

"His specialty," the **Denver Post** reported, "was a 'duffer' shot in which he leaped into the air and pushed the ball downward through the netting with a terrific swish."

Traditionalists found the dunk boring to watch, and critics said the stuff shot gave an unfair advantage to the new breed of taller players. After the 1966–67 season, the National Basketball Committee of the United States and Canada (a body of college coaches) banned all dunking or stuffing. The group's stated reasons: there's no defense against the dunk, which upsets the balance of the game; players can injure themselves; and dunking breaks backboards and bends rims.

In reality, the Alcindor Rule, as it came to be

called, was a sorry attempt by the coaching fraternity to keep UCLA from winning a second straight national title. UCLA's 7'1" center, Lew Alcindor (now Kareem Abdul-Jabbar), had averaged 29 points as a sophomore and led the Bruins to 30 straight victories and the 1967 national championship. That just wouldn't do; opposing coaches needed to cut Alcindor and UCLA down to size.

Did the no-dunk rule work? Well, in Alcindor's two remaining seasons in Westwood, UCLA lost just two games and won two more national titles. The rule forced Big Lew to perfect his jumper and develop a different shot that was virtually impossible to defend against—the sky hook.

After eight seasons, rule makers made dunking legal again in 1976. During a game that year, an overly excited Wiley Peck of Mississippi State dunked so hard that the ball came through the net and hit him in the face, knocking him cold for two minutes.

In 1979, Philadelphia 76ers center Darryl Dawkins shattered two backboards in 22 days with slam-dunks, thus inspiring the invention of the snap-back collapsible rim. Dawkins named his first dunk, which brought a hail of glass down on Bill Robinzine of the Kansas City Kings, the "Chocolate-Thunder Flyin', Robinzine-Cryin', Teeth-Shakin', Glass-Breakin', Rump-Roastin', Bun-Toastin', Wham, Bam, Glass-Breaker-I-Am-Jam."

For the record, the first woman to dunk in competition was Georgeann Wells. The 6'7" center for West Virginia made history during a 110–82 victory over the University of Charleston in 1984. "I made two or three dribbles," she would say later, "and then I took the glide."

# Which City Won the Most Titles in One Year?

**N**o city has won all four of the major sports championships (World Series, Super Bowl, NBA Finals, and Stanley Cup) in a single year. Pittsburgh, Pennsylvania, and New York City have come the closest. Each city has been home to two championship teams in one year.

The city of Pittsburgh enjoyed its championship season in 1979. That year, the Steelers won the

Super Bowl and the Pirates won the World Series.

New York City has accomplished the feat twice. In 1928, the Yankees won the World Series and the Rangers won the Stanley Cup. In 1969, the Jets won the Super Bowl and the Mets won the World Series.

Although no city has won three titles in the same year, New York came the closest, winning titles in three sports within the space of 17 months in 1969 and 1970. Joe Namath guaranteed that the Jets would beat the Colts in Super Bowl III, and on January 12, 1969, he and his teammates delivered. On October 16, 1969, another New York miracle occurred when the Amazin' Mets won the World Series over the Orioles. And on May 8, 1970, the Knicks beat the Lakers for the NBA title.

For being competitive across the board in a single 12-month period, the city that should rank the highest is Philadelphia. Between May 1980 and January 1981, the Phillies won their only World Series, the Flyers made the Stanley Cup finals and lost, the 76ers made the NBA Finals and lost, and the Eagles made the Super Bowl and lost. Knowing Philly fans, they probably thought it was their worst year ever.

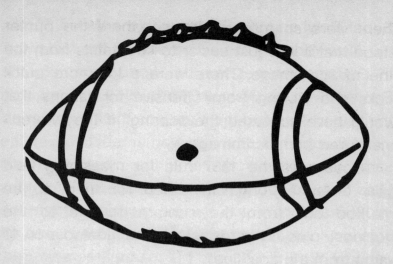

# Why Aren't Punts and Field Goals Measured the Same Way?

In football, the yardage for a punt is measured from the line of scrimmage. However, yardage for a field goal is measured from the point where the ball is placed to be kicked after the snap. When asked why the difference exists, Jack Reader, the NFL's assistant director of officiating, was thrown for a loss. "We don't know," he admitted. "It's just always been that way."

It seems that the punt rule dates to 1937, when official uniform statistics first were kept. Retired NCAA statistician Steve Boda says, "In those days there were so many variations where the punter stood that it was just easier to keep stats from the line of scrimmage. There were a lot more quick kicks and kicking from offensive formations that would have confused the scoring" if they weren't measured from scrimmage.

Boda says the 1937 rule for measuring field goal distances originally called for them to be marked off "from the scrimmage line to the goalpost plus 10 yards, since the goalpost is 10 yards from the goal line."

By the late 1950s, however, sportswriters and fans—apparently trying to make long kicks seem more impressive—often added the yardage from the point of placement. When it was written that "Smith kicked a 35-yard field goal," one couldn't be sure whether he booted the ball 35 yards from scrimmage (and thus 52 yards overall), or 35 yards from the spot where it was held.

The NCAA amended the rule in 1978, and field goals have been measured from the point of placement ever since. But even though punt distances have become standardized, they still are marked off from scrimmage.

# What Is the "Mendoza Line"?

**M**ario Mendoza was a slick-fielding but dreadfully weak-hitting shortstop for the Pittsburgh Pirates, Seattle Mariners, and Texas Rangers from 1974 to 1982. When he hit .198 as a regular for Seattle in 1979, teammates began referring to .200 as the "Mendoza Line." Soon major league players stopped saying that so-and-so couldn't hit his weight; now a feeble hitter had simply passed the Mendoza Line.

Mendoza says the term was invented by former Mariners teammate Tom Paciorek. Tom says, "It wasn't my idea. I think it was (former Mariner) Bruce Bochte's. I got the credit, but I don't want it."

Mendoza, whose lifetime average was .215, fell below the Mendoza Line in five of his nine seasons. Known as "El Aspirador"—Spanish for "the vacuum cleaner"—Mario was strictly a glove man. The native of Chihuahua, Mexico, made just 90 errors in 686 games.

In the early 1990s, Mario worked as a coach for Class A Palm Springs, a minor league rookie ball team owned by the California Angels. His job? Batting instructor. That's like having a vegetarian work at McDonald's!

## Who Started the 24-Second Shot Clock in Basketball?

The NBA's 24-second clock was the creation of Danny Biasone, who owned the Syracuse Nationals in the league's early days. (The Nats are now the Philadelphia 76ers.) The clock gives a team just 24 seconds to shoot the ball.

The NBA added the 24-second clock in 1954 to make the game more exciting. Before 1954, pro basketball was like a game of keep-away. Teams

would sometimes dribble and pass the ball for five minutes or longer without shooting; teams ahead in the fourth quarter would simply stall and run out the clock.

The low point came in November 1950, when the Fort Wayne Pistons held the ball for most of the game to defeat the Minneapolis Lakers 19–18. Fans grew bored of the stalling tactics and soon stopped buying tickets. The young league lost nine franchises over the next four years.

By the 1954–55 season (the league's ninth year), NBA owners searched for ways to speed up the game. They experimented with several rule changes, but none worked. So Danny developed his own idea of the shot clock. "Teams were taking about 60 shots in a game if nobody messed around," Danny said. "I figured if the teams combined for 120 shots in a game and the game was 48 minutes long...I divided 120 shots into 2,880 seconds. The answer was 24."

The clock may have saved pro basketball, yet it took Danny three years to persuade other owners to go along with his idea. Once they did, average team scores immediately rose 14 points to 93 points a game. Fans came back as the NBA's popularity soared. "The adoption of the clock," said league president Maurice Podoloff, "was the most important event in the NBA."

Danny, who died in May 1992, might someday be elected to the Basketball Hall of Fame (a special exhibit honors his accomplishment) but his invention of the shot clock did not go unrewarded at the time. In the final playoff game of the clock's first season, Danny's Nationals came from behind to win their only championship.

## What Is the Most Amazing Tackle in Football History?

In the second quarter of the 1954 Cotton Bowl game, Rice was leading Alabama 7–6 when Owls halfback Dickie Moegle broke loose for what looked like a sure touchdown run. Then, from out of nowhere, Alabama fullback Tommy Lewis tackled him. Lewis really did come from out of nowhere, because as Moegle sped down the sideline, Lewis was out of the game, sitting on the Crimson Tide bench.

When Lewis saw the game and the season slipping away from his team, he jumped off the bench and made the tackle as Moegle ran by. The officials ruled that Rice be awarded a 95-yard touchdown, and the Owls went on to win the game 28–6.

"I kept telling myself I didn't do it, but I knew I did," said Tommy. "I guess I'm too full of Alabama."

## Who Invented the Skateboard?

Skateboarding was invented by California surfers frustrated by bad waves. One day during the 1930s, when the surf wasn't up (or they couldn't get a ride to the beach), someone nailed roller-skate wheels to a two-by-four piece of wood and hit the sidewalks. A new sport was born. But nothing much happened with the sport until Frank Nasworthy introduced the plastic wheel in 1973.

The first skateboard wheels were made of wood, and were inexpensive, but they didn't last long enough to make skateboarding a practical sport. Then came the metal wheel commonly used on roller skates. But the metal wheels were loud and slippery while turning a corner, and if a skateboarder ever hit a rock or a pebble, the metal wheel stopped in its tracks and sent the rider flying.

By the mid-1960s, skateboards were made with wheels of hard clay. Unfortunately, whenever a rider cranked too hard into a sharp turn, the clay wheels gave way and dumped the rider to the ground.

Then one day Nasworthy was rummaging through a warehouse where barrels of plastic wheels had been stored since they had proved unsatisfactory for the roller rink. The plastic, called urethane, was softer than the metal or hard clay that wheels had been made of, and it gripped the road well. The warehouse owner gave Frank some wheels to use for his skateboards. After one ride, Frank realized that there might be a market for such a product. These wheels revolutionized the sport.

In 1973, Nasworthy introduced the first urethane wheels made especially for skateboards. Almost overnight the sport of skateboarding really started rolling. Today, according to Don Bostick, president of the National Skateboard Association, there are 10 million skaters in the United States.

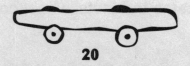

# How Many Dimples Are on a Golf Ball?

**W**ould you believe 324? Or maybe 384? Or even 440?

Before we get to these numbers we first must go through a little "dimpleology." By the 1890s golfers had discovered that a ball flew up to 60 percent longer and a whole lot truer if it had been nicked here and there. So manufacturers built iron molds and presses to turn out balls with tiny **raised** bumps in concentric circles. Dimples came in 1908 when it became apparent that they were aerodynamically better than bumps.

The size, number, and pattern of dimples, as it turns out, all have a lot to do with a ball's carrying distance and trajectory. The deeper the dimple, for example, the lower the ball will go; the shallower the dimple, the higher the ball will go. There's no magic number of dimples a ball should have because dimple **coverage** (how much of the ball is dimpled) is more important than dimple count.

Until 1984 most golf balls had 324 or 336 dimples (why anyone took the time to count them is a mystery). Greater dimple coverage increases carrying distance, so Titleist that year introduced a ball with 384 dimples. One of Titleist's newer products, the HVC, has 440 dimples of eleven different sizes.

## Who Started the Fast Break?

The originator of the fast break was Frank Keaney, coach of Rhode Island State from 1921 to 1947. The break was a strategy born of desperation, for Coach Keaney's teams had no size. But they were quick and could shoot, and the 1936 Rhode Island State team (the Firehouse Gang, or the Runnin' Rams, as they were known) averaged 51 points when the center jump after every basket was eliminated.

That doesn't sound like much scoring today, but the point-a-minute pace was breathlessly reported in the press. Keaney's players charged down court after every rebound or basket, hauling in long passes to the amazement of fans. His teams also were some of the first to use the full-court press on defense.

Keaney was a master amateur psychologist. Wanting to prepare the team to run in smoke-filled Madison Square Garden in 1946, when Rhode Island was in the National Invitational Tournament (the equivalent of today's NCAA tournament), Keaney had students collect cigarette and cigar butts for weeks. He then burned them in a barrel during practice, thoroughly acclimating the players.

## What Is the Most Efficient Game Ever Pitched?

Righthander Red Barrett of the Boston Braves needed just 58 pitches—an incredible 6.4 pitches per inning—to shut out the Cincinnati Reds 2–0, on August 10, 1944. The game, played before 7,783 fans at Crosley Field, lasted 1 hour and 15 minutes.

Barrett allowed two hits, walked none, and struck out none (walks and strikeouts, don't forget, do use up pitches). Most teams toward the end of World War II were patched together, many of the stars having gone overseas, and the box score of Barrett's game contains few well-known names. The best hitter he faced was first baseman Frank McCormick.

Barrett had a lifetime record of 69–69 with the Reds, Braves, and Cardinals. His catcher in 1944 was Stew Hofferth. The redheaded Barrett "pitched real fast, he didn't wait around," recalled Hofferth. "He was throwing right down the middle and the Reds kept hitting the first pitch—mostly popups and ground balls."

## Which College Football Team Gave Back a Win?

In a game played between Dartmouth and Cornell in November 1940, with less than two minutes to go and Dartmouth ahead 3–0, Cornell had the ball at the Dartmouth 6-yard line. The Indians held for three straight downs, and Cornell inadvertently committed a delay-of-game penalty.

Walter Scholl of the Big Red then failed to connect on a pass into the end zone, and with six seconds left, Dartmouth fans began celebrating. Referee Red Friesell, however, signaled that one more down remained. Scholl then completed another end-zone pass for a touchdown and the win.

After reviewing game films, Friesell, who had become confused by the penalty, recognized his mistake and formally apologized to Dartmouth. His admission of error, though, did not change the score. Only when Cornell's president, athletic director, and coach agreed that such a victory was not worth keeping did the score go down in the record books as a 3–0 loss to Dartmouth.

A similar mix-up occurred in October 1990 when national co-champion-to-be Colorado used a fifth down against Missouri to score a touchdown for a come-from-behind victory with two seconds left. The Big 8 Conference, however, refused to reverse the game's outcome, and Colorado declined to relinquish the victory.

# In Hockey, Why Are Three Goals by a Single Player Called a "Hat Trick"?

"Hat trick" first came into usage around 1875 in cricket. In that sport the term refers to the dismissal by the bowler of three batters with three straight pitches. According to **Webster's Sports Dictionary,** the bowler got a new hat whenever he accomplished this rare feat.

Most U.S. sports fans use the term in hockey. European fans use the term in soccer, too. The term came into use in the U.S. in the mid-1950s. In both sports it originally meant the scoring of three unanswered goals by one player in a single game. Somewhere along the line (NHL expansion?) the meaning must have grown foggy, because the goals no longer need to be unanswered to qualify.

At NHL games, hockey fans toss hats onto the ice to celebrate a hat trick. At some games, as many as 100 hats are scattered across the rink. Of course, making 100 hats disappear is a different kind of hat trick! Arena workers pick up the caps and pile them in wheelbarrows to be taken away.

What to do with so many hats? The Philadelphia Flyers keep their hat-trick collection in a glass case in their home arena, CoreStates Center. The case contains more than 200 hats. The team has another 400 hats in storage! The Boston Bruins donate their hats to a local youth-hockey league. The Colorado Avalanche let fans take back their hats after the game. Most other NHL teams simply throw the hats away.

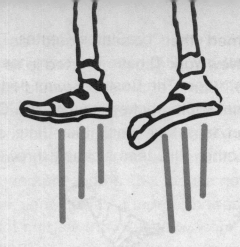

# Who Took the First Jump Shot in Basketball?

**F**orward Hank Luisetti of Stanford was the man, and his running one-handed jumper, released from just off his right ear, transformed the game of basketball.

The date was December 30, 1936. Stanford had come east to play Clair Bee's Long Island University team, winner of 43 straight games, at Madison Square Garden. Stanford blew out the Pioneers 45–31, and Hank, shooting his jumper on the move from that weird angle, scored 15 points—an impressive total in those days.

"It seemed that Luisetti could do nothing wrong," the **New York Times** reported in its account of the game. "Some of his shots would have been deemed foolhardy if attempted by anybody else."

Until Hank's jumper, basketball had known only two kinds of shots: the layup and the two-handed set shot. Soon school kids across the country were firing one-handed jumpers just off their ears. "We didn't really know what we were starting that night," says Hank, now retired and living in Burlingame, California.

Around that time, a boy named Kenny Sailors took notice of Luisetti's bold technique. Kenny grew up in Wyoming playing basketball against his older brother, Bud. But Bud kept blocking Kenny's shots, and Kenny grew frustrated. Soon, Kenny discovered that he could successfully shoot over his taller, older brother by jumping as he shot, holding the ball with one hand high above his head.

Kenny's accurate jump shot helped the University of Wyoming win the 1943 NCAA championship. He scored 16 points in the final game and was named the tournament's Most Outstanding Player. By the 1950s, almost every basketball player was shooting the jumper (later to be called the "J").

# Who Ran the
# Most Embarrassing Mile Race?

For a distance runner, it's not how you start, it's how you finish. But finish you must, if you want to win.

From 1987 to 1990, Suzy Favor Hamilton of the University of Wisconsin was a top collegiate miler, winning a record nine NCAA titles. In 1991 she won the U.S. championship at that same distance. In a 1994 mile event, she tested her ability against the world's best, Algeria's Hassiba Boulmerka, the reigning Olympic gold medalist and world champion.

Although she trailed in the first half-mile, Suzy was determined to lead the pack. She gained steadily until finally she and Hassiba were neck-and-neck with two laps to go. Then Suzy sprinted to the front, seemingly on her way to a spectacular upset. But she suddenly stopped running and screamed, "Oh, no!"

Suzy wasn't hurt, yet she couldn't finish the race, and Hassiba breezed to victory. An indoor mile is eight trips around the oval. Unfortunately, Suzy miscounted and stopped running after seven laps. She later explained that she was concentrating so hard on winning that she forgot to keep count.

"I'm a college graduate," she says. "It was the

weirdest feeling. I couldn't believe it. I was shocked. I wanted to say, 'Everybody stop.' I wanted to jump back in."

## What Is the Most Embarrassing Moment in Olympic History?

In Atlanta at the 1996 Summer Olympic Games, Dani Tyler learned an important lesson: Always watch where you're going.

The 21-year-old third baseman for the U.S. women's softball team smacked a home run against Australia in the fifth inning of a scoreless game. But in her excitement to high-five a teammate, Dani leaped over home plate without touching it. When the Aussies appealed, the umpire called Dani out.

The U.S. team lost in extra innings for only their second international defeat in ten years. Dani felt awful. "I didn't want to get out of bed the next morning," she said.

Despite the heart-breaking defeat, the U.S. team recovered to win the gold medal. Dani also rallied. "One play won't define my life. What happened was a freak thing. It's over. If I whine about it, or make excuses, or argue with the umpire, I'll look like a jerk," she said, adding, "From now on, I'll put a big 'X-marks-the-spot' on home plate and step on it with both feet."

The most embarrassing moment in the history of the Winter Olympics occurred at the 1992 Games in Albertville, France. Most Olympians will always remember their moment on the world stage, but Alexandre Bortiuk would rather forget.

Alex, a pusher on the Soviets' Unified Team's four-man bobsled, went for a backwards ride on the second run. Alex stumbled at the end of the push-off and fought with all his might to get on board the moving sled. But he landed back-to-back with the driver, placing him face-to-face with another teammate! The seating mistake caused a very slow ride for the Unified Team's sled, which finished in nineteenth place after the four runs.

# Why Is the NFL's Championship Game Called the "Super Bowl"?

The first two Super Bowl games in 1967 and 1968 were called the "AFL-NFL World Championship Game." That terrible tongue-twister was Commissioner Pete Rozelle's idea. "I guess coming up with catchy names wasn't something I was very good at," said Rozelle.

Lamar Hunt, the owner of the AFL Kansas City Chiefs, got the idea to name the game the "Super Bowl" from his daughter's favorite toy: the Super Ball. "I was just kidding at first when I mentioned the Super Bowl in meetings," said Hunt. "But then the other owners started using it and the press started picking it up."

Commissioner Rozelle didn't like the name, saying, "To me, 'super' was a corny cliché word." Thankfully, Hunt convinced the other team owners to adopt the name. The term **"Super Bowl"** became official in 1969 with Super Bowl III.

The use of Roman numerals actually began with

Super Bowl V, which was won by the Baltimore Colts over the Dallas Cowboys 16–13 on Jim O'Brien's 32-yard field goal with five seconds remaining. The Roman numerals were adopted to clear up any confusion that might occur because the Super Bowl is played in January of the next year following a season. Numerals I through IV were added to the first four Super Bowls afterward.

By the way, a ticket to the first Super Bowl played in January 1967 cost $12. For anyone who wants to attend Super Bowl XXXIV, a ticket will set you back over $200.

## What Is the Most Determined Performance by a Jockey?

Jockey Nate Hubbard literally hung on for second place during a horse race at California's Golden Gate Fields in 1989.

Nate was riding Sweetwater Oak when the horse clipped heels with eventual winner Current Lady with a sixteenth of a mile to go and sent him flying out of the saddle. Nate held on to the neck of his horse and was afraid to let go.

"When she almost fell, I grabbed a handful of mane and held on," said Nate. "I was afraid I would get run over."

Nate's arms hugged the horse's neck and his legs dangled for 20 seconds as Sweetwater Oak crossed the finish line in second place. Officials allowed the second place result because rules state a horse must carry the required weight across the finish line and Nate never touched the ground.

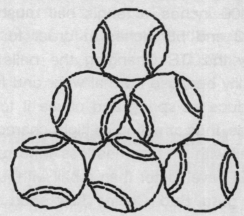

# How Often Are Tennis Balls Changed in a Pro Match?

**N**ew balls are put into play after the first seven games of a match, and following every nine games thereafter. The balls used in the first seven games also are used in the five-minute warm-up period before the match, which is the equivalent of about two games. Balls are not changed at the start of tie-breakers.

The International Tennis Federation, which establishes the rules for ball changes, also requires that six balls be used at any one time. (Can you imagine how the tongues of those 14-year-old ball kids would be hanging out if only two were used?)

When dropped upon a concrete base from a height of 100 inches, a tennis ball must bounce between 53 and 58 inches in order to become certified by the ITF. Changing the balls assures bounce-ability because normal wear and tear on a ball will reduce its spring and cause it to lose its fuzzy surface, thus affecting its flight characteristics. A tennis ball with no fuzz has less wind resistance and thus will travel faster than a ball with full fuzz.

Tennis guru Bud Collins has seen matches played on wet grass courts in which the tournament director ordered that new balls be used after the first five games, and then after every seven games. Tennis balls that absorb water will weigh more and cause the ball to play "heavy."

# Who Started the Spike in Football?

The first spike of a football in an NFL game occurred on October 17, 1965. The innovator was New York Giants receiver Homer Jones. It happened in the second quarter of a game against the Philadelphia Eagles. Homer scored on an 89-yard pass from quarterback Earl Morrall.

It was Homer's first NFL touchdown, and he wanted to celebrate. Homer was about to heave the ball to the cheering crowd—but the NFL fined players for throwing the ball into the stands. "That would have cost me five hundred dollars," says Homer. "So I threw the ball down as hard as I could."

From 1965 to 1969, Homer earned a reputation as one of the fastest, most dangerous players in football. During those five standout seasons with the Giants, he once led the NFL in touchdowns, four times led it in average yardage per catch, and was named to the Pro Bowl and All-NFL teams.

But it was actually during his college playing days at Texas Southern that Homer developed his showmanship—that of slamming the football to the ground after scoring a touchdown. It happened in a game against Southern University.

"I ran for a 70-yard touchdown and a Southern linebacker said: 'Okay, Superman, try it again.' Then I ran a counter play for an 80-yard touchdown. I threw the ball down and I told him, 'There's the ball, now here's Superman.' I just threw it down real hard. And it just got to be a habit."

Soon other players started copying Homer's simple spike. Today, almost all touchdowns are punctuated by this scoring celebration—and more!

The first NFL touchdown dance happened in 1971. Elmo Wright, the Kansas City Chiefs receiver, sprinted into the end zone and started an exaggerated run in place. It was kind of a high-stomping act with his knees rising chest-high. When he finished after a few seconds, he spiked the ball.

In 1974, Billy "White Shoes" Johnson of the Houston Oilers celebrated his TDs with a dance called the "Funky Chicken." After a score, Billy would wiggle his legs as if they were made of rubber while holding the ball over his head.

Other memorable celebrations have been performed by Ickey Woods of the Cincinnati Bengals (the "Ickey Shuffle"), Butch Johnson of the Dallas Cowboys (the "California Quake"), and the "Fun Bunch" Washington Redskins receivers.

# How Was an NBA Game Rained Out?

The first rainout in the NBA's always-indoor history occurred on January 5, 1986, in a game between the Seattle SuperSonics and the Phoenix Suns. The game was called during the second quarter with the Suns leading 35–24. Cause of the rainout: a hole in the roof of the Seattle Coliseum.

Actually, the game was canceled because of a leaky roof that was dripping water on the floor, making for slippery and dangerous conditions. The leak had been discovered early that morning by stadium workers, who placed plastic tarps on the roof to prevent any further seepage.

Unfortunately, heavy winds blew away the tarps, and by game time, water spots began forming on the court. When the water began collecting at one end of the floor, fans started chanting "Half court. Half court." When the leak got worse, play was stopped. After an hour delay, officials decided to call off the game. And the NBA experienced its first ever rainout.

When the teams met again the next night to complete the game, Phoenix beat Seattle 114–97.

# Who Is Responsible for Creating the Designated Hitter?

Former major league manager Bobby Bragan is considered the father of the designated hitter. In 1973, Bragan—then president of the Texas League and a member of baseball's rules committee—put the DH on the panel's agenda for a vote. From 1970 to 1972, the American League had averaged only 12 million fans per year in attendance (less than 75 percent of National League attendance), so Commissioner Bowie Kuhn and AL president Joe Cronin thought the DH would be a quick fix. The proposal passed as a three-year AL "experiment."

A similar rule to the DH rule was first proposed in 1929 by National League president John Heydler, but the AL then considered it ridiculous.

Interestingly, it cannot be demonstrated that the DH ever helped AL attendance. But getting rid of this "experiment" will be as hard as stamping out artificial turf. Baseball's current commissioner, Bud Selig, seems to be against the DH, but AL owners and the Players' Association would have to approve any repeal, and union leaders are not likely to abolish million-dollar jobs currently being held by dues-paying members.

For the record, Ron Blomberg of the New York Yankees made baseball history when he stepped into the batter's box on Opening Day in 1973. The Yankees were playing the Red Sox in Fenway Park when, in the first inning, Blomberg became the first DH to bat in a major league game.

Blomberg, who faced Boston pitcher Luis Tiant with the bases loaded, drew a walk and forced in a Yankee run. The first major league plate appearance by a designated hitter was not an official at-bat, although Blomberg was credited with a run batted in. The DH rule wasted no time adding offense to the game!

# What Is the Most Popular Sports Rally Song?

It's been said that music calms the savage breast—and when combined with the fast-paced, unpredictable tempo of sports, music also excites and invigorates. Professional and college teams throughout the country use music to get the crowd fired up to fever pitch.

One foot-stomping tune that resonates in stadiums and arenas is **Rock and Roll, Part 2** by Gary Glitter. This popular hit from the 1960s has once again returned to the top of the charts like a bullet, thanks to its heavy play at sporting events.

The song's national coming-out party occurred during the 1991 World Series at the Metrodome in Minnesota. It was played over the public address system when the home team Twins scored a run. It really stoked the crowd by letting them chant "Hey" in unison on every other fourth beat.

The song had originally become popular in the Twin Cities earlier that spring when the North Stars reached the Stanley Cup finals. When the Twins reached the American League playoffs, Joe Johnston—then the team's game production manager—decided to play the number.

"It's a crowd-pleaser, a real rally song," Johnston said. "The fans automatically related to the music, and when they yelled 'Hey!' and the homer hankies flew, it was awesome."

Another sports rally song that is at least semi-awesome is **We Will Rock You/We Are the Champions** by the rock group Queen, which is sung at a number of stadiums, and **Na Na Hey Hey Kiss Him Goodbye,** a Comiskey Park favorite since 1969.

**Na Na Hey Hey Kiss Him Goodbye** was a one-hit wonder by a band named Steam. It generally is used to serenade knocked-out pitchers for the other side. Comiskey Park organist Nancy Faust, who in 1969 was a rookie fresh out of college, played the song simply because she liked it. Now all of Southside Chicago likes it.

# Which High School Produces the Most NBA Players?

**D**eMatha High in Hyattsville, Maryland, has sent 12 players to the NBA. Official statistics on this subject aren't kept by the league, but we'd be surprised if DeMatha, long a pipeline for the NBA, doesn't hold the record.

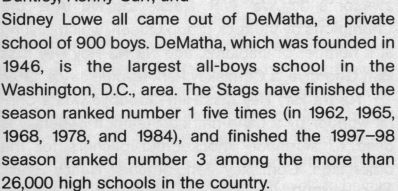

Danny Ferry, Adrian Dantley, Kenny Carr, and Sidney Lowe all came out of DeMatha, a private school of 900 boys. DeMatha, which was founded in 1946, is the largest all-boys school in the Washington, D.C., area. The Stags have finished the season ranked number 1 five times (in 1962, 1965, 1968, 1978, and 1984), and finished the 1997–98 season ranked number 3 among the more than 26,000 high schools in the country.

DeMatha has been coached since 1956 by Morgan Wooten, the all-time winningest high school basketball coach (career record: 1,153–170). Coach

Wooten says every one of his seniors between 1957 and 1991 was offered a college athletic scholarship. The man's influence on the sport is evident by the fact that eight of Wooten's former players and assistant coaches are currently head coaches at Division I-A basketball programs.

## What Is the "Sneakers Game"?

No, it's not the athletic-shoe wars between Nike and Adidas. The 1934 NFL Championship Game between the New York Giants and the Chicago Bears became known as the "Sneakers Game" because the Giants' players exchanged their football cleats for sneakers.

Prior to the game, Chicago was heavily favored to win their third straight championship. The Bears were undefeated in 13 regular season games (having outscored opponents 286–86) and had already beaten the Giants twice.

The title game on December 9, 1934, was played at New York's Polo Grounds in frigid weather. Players were slipping and sliding on the frozen field because their cleats couldn't dig into the rock-hard turf. Both teams were playing poorly, but the Bears had built a 10–3 halftime lead on a Bronko Nagurski touchdown run and a Jack Manders field goal.

That's when Giants coach Steve Owen told equipment man Abe Cohen to search for shoes that would give his players better traction on the icy field. Abe left the stadium and rushed to Manhattan College, where he collected boxes and boxes of sneakers from the basketball players' locker room.

By the time Abe returned with the sneakers, the Bears had added another field goal and led 13–3 in the fourth quarter. The Giants players quickly put on their sneakers, and the game changed immediately. The Giants were now able to cut and turn on the slippery surface. The sure-footed Giants ran past the Bears for 27 unanswered points in the final 10 minutes and won the game 30–13. It was New York's first NFL championship.

# What's the Best Bowling Series Ever Recorded?

Jeremy Sonnenfeld bowled the best three-game series recognized by the American Bowling Congress. Jeremy, a 20-year-old University of Nebraska student, made history in February 1997 when he became the first bowler to roll a 900 series in the 101-year history of the ABC.

Jeremy, a sophomore business major from Sioux Falls, South Dakota, rolled three consecutive 300 games—that's 36 straight strikes!—at Sun Valley Lanes during a fund-raising tournament for the Nebraska bowling team.

What made the score even more amazing was how Jeremy did it. Because of the tournament format, Jeremy bowled on six different lanes instead of the usual two.

The previous three-game record was 899, shared by three bowlers. So when Jeremy headed to the tenth frame of his third game, Sun Valley Lanes came to a halt. "It was totally quiet," recalled Jeremy. "When I threw a strike on my first ball, everybody cheered."

Using his 16-pound, Columbia Pearlized Pulse

ball, Jeremy found the pocket again on his final ball, scattering all ten pins. "The place went crazy and people started carrying me around on their shoulders," said Jeremy. "It was unreal."

As for the Women's International Bowling Congress, the highest three-game series was 877 in tournament play by Jackie Mitskavich of Dubois, Pennsylvania, in August 1997. Jackie is on the Ladies Pro Bowlers Tour.

The ABC acknowledges that at least four other 900 series have been reported before Jeremy's feat, but none was officially approved by the ABC because of lane conditions. The quality of lanes, which depends in part on the amount of oil used on them, definitely can make a difference.

ABC specifications allow bowling lanes, which are 60 feet long, to be oiled anywhere from 24 to 40 feet beyond the foul line, but never near the pins. When traveling on the oiled part of the lane, a ball lacks grip and thus moves in a relatively straight line. The ball doesn't start hooking until it reaches the "dry" or unoiled wood. Oil is usually added to the middle of the lanes to help balls stay away from the gutter.

# What Happens to Old Stadiums?

**E**very great ballplayer must someday hang up his spikes, and every great stadium must eventually sit empty or yield to the wrecking ball.

Toronto's not-so-great Exhibition Stadium, the Blue Jays' home from 1977 to 1989—and the site where Dave Winfield accidentally killed a seagull with a thrown ball in 1983—has not been razed. The seagull center still is the site of concerts (in 1997 it hosted U2 and Bon Jovi) and other events.

Minnesota's Metropolitan Stadium, home of the Twins from 1961 to 1981, faced an even more dramatic fate than hosting thousands of screaming teenagers. It was demolished in 1984, and the Mall of America—the world's largest shopping center— has been built in its place.

A number of other storied parks are long gone, too. Ebbets Field in Brooklyn and the Polo Grounds in New York, which were leveled by the same wrecking ball in 1960 and 1964, respectively, are now the homes of public-housing projects. Connie Mack Stadium in Philadelphia and old Busch Stadium in St. Louis are vacant lots.

Some old ballfields have been memorialized.

The site of Forbes Field is now part of the University of Pittsburgh campus; the centerfield wall still stands and home plate sits beneath a piece of Lucite set in the floor of the Forbes Quadrangle. Whole sections of Cincinnati's Crosley Field have been moved to a ballfield in Blue Ash, Ohio, where charity and commemorative games are sometimes played.

As for Memorial Stadium in Baltimore, the city's plan to maintain the park in hopes that an NFL franchise would find its way to town has worked. The former Cleveland Browns have become the Baltimore Ravens, replacing the Colts, who fled under cover of night in 1983, but it's still not the same as when the Colts played there.

## What Is the Most Surprising Practical Joke Ever Played?

There were three games left in the 1987 season, and the Williamsport (Pennsylvania) Bills were in seventh place in the Class AA Eastern League—28 games out of first place. Catcher Dave Bresnahan was bored and wanted to stir things up, so he peeled a potato before a game against Reading and kept it in a spare catcher's mitt in the dugout.

In the fifth inning, with a runner on third base, Dave told the home plate umpire he needed to change mitts. When Dave came back he had the potato hidden in his glove. As the pitch came in, he switched the potato to his throwing hand, caught the ball and then threw the potato wildly over the head of the third baseman.

When the Reading runner saw what he thought was the ball rolling into left field, he came jogging home, but was tagged out at the plate by Bresnahan. Because baseball rules state that you cannot fool a runner, the umpire called the runner safe. Dave's team was so mad at the stunt that he was released the next day. Surprised, Bresnahan said he was "just trying to put some fun into the game. I mean, it's not like it was the seventh game of the World Series."

# Who Has Been on the Most Sports Illustrated Covers?

**M**ichael Jordan rules **SI**'s roost, having appeared on the cover 42 times as of the March 2, 1998, issue. Muhammad Ali is second with 34 cover appearances. In third place is Kareem Abdul-Jabbar with 28 covers. Tied for fourth are Magic Johnson and Jack Nicklaus with 23 covers each. Next on the list are Larry Bird (20) and fallen hero Pete Rose (17).

Who has the best chance of catching Jordan? Tiger Woods is a strong candidate, but his cover appearances are also dependent on his future success on the golf links.

For the record, **SI**'s first cover on August 16, 1954, featured Eddie Mathews of the Braves (along with New York Giants catcher Wes Westrum and umpire Augie Donatelli). They were pictured in a tableau of a night game at Milwaukee County Stadium. Mathews, a Hall of Famer-to-be, appeared on the cover once more, in 1958.

# How Are College Football Polls Decided?

**T**he Associated Press (AP) poll, which has been around since 1936, consists of a panel of 70 sportswriters representing such influential journals as the **Kalamazoo** (Michigan) **Gazette** and the **Laramie** (Wyoming) **Daily Boomerang.** Voting rights are given only to newspapers in states that play Division I-A college football. So media types based in Connecticut and North Dakota, for instance, do not vote.

The **USA Today**/ESPN coaches' poll—begun in 1950 as the United Press International (UPI) poll—consists of 62 Division I-A coaches. The coaches' poll also seems to have an unbalanced membership. For example, in 1991, Gary Blackney, then rookie coach of Bowling Green, was a member; Penn State coaching legend Joe Paterno was not.

Both polls require their members to call in their choices on Sunday. (AP's deadline is 2 o'clock, says Paul Montella, who oversees the wire service poll, "which means that by then 15 of our 70 writers will have phoned in.") The balloting is inherently controversial. Some coaches have low-balled their own teams and rated their opponents unusually high the week before big games. And sports information directors at some colleges have been known to fill out a coach's ballot.

"Beauty is in the eye of the beholder," says former Nebraska coach Tom Osborne. "Who knows why people vote the way they do?"

In 1997, Michigan (12–0) was number 1 in the AP poll and Nebraska (13–0) was number 1 in the **USA Today**/ESPN coaches' poll. It was the third time in the 1990s that the national title was shared. The other split polls occurred in 1990 (Colorado was the AP champion and Georgia Tech number 1 in the coaches' poll) and 1991 (Miami was number 1 in the AP poll while the coaches chose Washington).

Although many believe the poll difference is good for college football, some think the recent run of co-champions points out the need for a playoff system. But many coaches like the bowl process because it allows 20 teams to end their seasons with a postseason victory. Tradition, politics, and big-money bowl sponsors also stand in the way of a playoff tournament.

# What Is a "Texas Leaguer"?

**A** "Texas Leaguer" is a fly ball that falls just beyond the reach of an infielder and in front of an outfielder for a base hit. The term goes back to the 1800s and a player named Art Sunday, who was a star hitter for Houston of the Texas League. In 1890, Sunday hit .398 for Toledo of the International League. Many of his hits were short flies that fell safely. A Toledo sportswriter kept referring to them as "Texas League hits." Soon they came to be known as "Texas Leaguers."

Texas Leaguers, or "flares," as players call them today, usually are accidental, but decades ago some hitters became skilled at blooping the ball between the infielders and outfielders.

There is evidence to suggest that these hits, originally called "plunkers," were favored as trick plays in the Texas League because fences generally were far away from the plate and outfielders played deep. Sunday may have been the game's greatest plunker.

# Who Started the Wishbone Offense in Football?

The Wishbone is a variation of the T-formation in which the halfbacks line up farther from the line of scrimmage than the fullback, giving the backfield the appearance of a wishbone. The Wishbone made its debut at the University of Texas in 1968 when Darrell Royal was the coach.

Royal wanted to switch to a fullhouse backfield because he had three excellent running backs. He credits Assistant Coach Emory Bellard with developing the Wishbone. Bellard's fondness for the Triple Option inspired the offense, but the Wishbone contains ideas from several sources.

The fake handoff to the fullback from a Triple Option formation had been used by Gene Henderson at Nedland, Texas, High School. That play was based on the University of Houston Veer, a Triple Option out of the I-formation. Coach Royal also saw an effective—but infrequently called—fake handoff to the fullback used by Gene Stallings at Texas A&M in 1967.

On September 21, 1968, against Houston, Texas unveiled an offense using the fullback close to the quarterback like A&M. But Bellard later moved the fullback two steps back and split the tailbacks to either side instead of stacking them.

This offense was briefly called the "Y"-formation, but sportswriter Mickey Herskowitz of the **Houston Post** dubbed it the "Wishbone-T." With only a tight end and one split end, the offense is designed for running instead of passing.

Texas won the national title in 1969 and 30 consecutive games with the formation before losing to Notre Dame in the Cotton Bowl at the end of the 1970 season.

# What Is a Long-Distance Swim Meet?

Purdue swam by phone in January 1978 against Indiana State because a snowstorm would otherwise have wiped out the meet.

Before Purdue boarded the bus for the 100-mile trip from West Lafayette, Indiana, to Terre Haute, a blizzard struck. The Boilermakers had already been snowed out of six meets that season and Indiana State was sympathetic, so coaches Fred Kahms of Purdue and Duane Barrows of ISU put their heads together.

They hit upon the idea of a phone meet. Barrows called Kahms at Purdue and kept the line open for 2 hours, 15 minutes (total bill: $25). Before each race Kahms and Barrows identified to each other their respective swimmers. The coaches then went to their pools for the race and came back on the line with exact times so the order of finish could be calculated.

"Each school had all the same officials they would have at a regular competition," said Kahms, who retired in 1985. "We had timers, referees, a starter and even a public address announcer who would tell the fans before each race who the swimmers were supposed to be in the empty lanes."

In the diving half of the meet, each school used its own judges. Indiana State won that competition by a half-point, but Purdue won the meet 68–45.

In January 1990, Cornell and Princeton also held a long-distance swim meet when a blizzard struck Ithaca, New York. Times do change. This one was conducted by fax machine.

# What Is Meant by a "Player to Be Named Later"?

"**A** player to be named later" is used to describe an undetermined player in a trade. For example, Team A agrees to send a player to Team B. Team A will receive a player in return, but his identity will be decided in the future. When the deal is announced, the clubs state that it involves a "player to be named later."

Harry Dalton, former general manager of the Milwaukee Brewers, said the term is used as a "delay to allow waivers to be secured for the player agreed upon." He also said that sometimes a pool of three or four players will be created so they can be scouted before one is chosen.

In the most famous such trade, the 1962 New York Mets acquired catcher Harry Chiti—who was the property of the Cleveland Indians and playing for their Jacksonville farm club—for a "player to be named later."

After Chiti caught a few games for his new team, his lack of talent was obvious, and the Mets were ready to unload him. They still owed a player to the Indians, so they sent Chiti back to Jacksonville.

The trade was Chiti for Chiti! The Mets had traded a player for himself.

In a deal in 1985, the San Francisco Giants got David Green, Gary Rajsich, Dave LaPoint, and Jose Gonzalez from the St. Louis Cardinals in exchange for Jack Clark. After joining the Giants, Gonzalez changed his last name to Uribe, his mother's maiden name, because two other pro shortstops were named Jose Gonzalez. This prompted Giants coach Rocky Bridges to say, "Jose was truly the player to be named later in the trade."

# When Was TV's First Instant Replay?

The first television instant replay occurred on December 7, 1963, during the annual Army-Navy game, won by Navy 21–15. Tony Verna (what other initials could he have?) was a young director for CBS who introduced the new concept of showing a play again immediately after it had been seen by the television audience.

With a Cotton Bowl bid at stake for the winner, number 2-ranked Navy led Army 21–7 in the fourth quarter. Less than seven minutes remained when Cadet quarterback Rollie Stichweh faked a handoff, scored on a bootleg, and then ran for a two-point conversion, pulling Army to within six points. In its broadcast of the game, CBS made the touchdown run TV's first instant replay.

So strange was the idea of seeing a play again just seconds after it had occurred that Lindsey Nelson, who was announcing the game, had to warn viewers that they were not seeing things. "This is not live!" Nelson screamed into the microphone. "Ladies and gentlemen, Army did not score again!"

The touchdown would be the only time that day CBS used instant replay because the replay pictures were not very clear. Still, the innovation forever changed the way we watch televised sports.

# Who Has the Most Explosive Slapshot?

**M**embers of the University of Michigan women's field hockey team were freezing during a game against Northwestern in November 1996. The wind-chill factor made the game-time temperature drop below zero. But senior attacker Michelle Smulders was hot.

The Wolverines' leading scorer had netted two second-half goals to tie the game. Michelle's father was in the bleachers rooting for her. "My dad likes to yell 'KA-BOOM!' when I shoot," said Michelle.

Near game's end, Michigan was awarded a penalty corner. This is a free hit from 16 yards away. Michelle usually took the penalty corners because of her powerful shot. When Michelle smacked the hard plastic ball, her father once again yelled "KA-BOOM!" This time, however, Michelle heard another sound. "I thought my stick broke," she said.

Instead, it was the ball that broke in two pieces! One half rolled out of bounds, and the opposing goalie made a save on the other half. "Everyone was confused," said Michelle. "What would've happened if the ball went in the net? Would I have scored half a goal?"

# What Is the
# Most Exciting Car Race Ever?

Racing is in Al Unser, Jr.'s, blood. His father, Al Unser, Sr., has won the Indianapolis 500 four times; his uncle Bobby has won three times. At Indy in 1992, it was Little Al's turn.

This particular Indy was scarred with accidents. Of the 33 cars to start the race, only 12 would finish. Little Al was careful to stay out of trouble, as was the driver who started in last place, Scott Goodyear. After 190 of the 200 laps, the two were neck and neck. Al was in first place, but Scott was just off his back fender.

Scott searched desperately for a way to pass Al. He tried to go high on the straightaways, then low on the turns. But Al, at 220 m.p.h., smartly swerved his car from side to side, refusing to allow Scott room to pass.

With 100 yards to go, Scott swept inside Al's car in a final effort to snatch victory. It was not enough.

Little Al took the checkered flag a heartbeat ahead of Scott, winning by .043 of a second. After racing for 500 miles, Little Al was about half a car length better than Scott. It was the closest finish ever at the Indy 500.

# Who Is the Real "Mean Gene" Okerlund?

It's often difficult to separate fact from fiction in professional wrestling, but here goes:

In the late 1970s, Gene Okerlund was working as a television advertising salesman for MetroMedia in Minneapolis when the on-air announcers for the local American Wrestling Association went on strike. He filled in and soon gained a cult following with his fast talk and cornball overacting.

Dubbed "Mean Gene" by AWA wrestler Jesse (The Body) Ventura, Okerlund went national with his close friend Hulk Hogan in 1983 when World Wrestling Federation owner Vince McMahon raided talent from other wrestling organizations. In real life the bombastic Okerlund is chairman of an advertising agency that has handled such accounts as Sam Goody Records and SAS Airlines.

## What Is the Most Embarrassing Moment in Football History?

Former Minnesota Vikings defensive lineman Jim Marshall owns the NFL record for playing in 282 consecutive games. But there's one game—against the San Francisco 49ers during the 1964 season— he probably wishes he'd left early.

In the third quarter, a 49er player fumbled. Jim scooped up the loose ball and started running toward the end zone. His teammates began yelling at him. Jim thought they were cheering him on. Defensive players rarely touch the ball, much less score touchdowns. But in all the excitement, Jim had gotten confused. He cruised 66 yards into the end zone—the wrong way!

"I knew something was wrong," he says, "when a 49er player gave me a hug."

Jim's wrong-way dash resulted in a two-point safety for San Francisco, but Minnesota won anyway 27–22. When he returned home after the game, Jim received hundreds of telephone calls from supportive friends.

"I still feel embarrassed about that play, and I suppose I'll never be allowed to forget it," says Jim, who played in four Super Bowls. "But I don't see any reason to hide, either. If people want to laugh, I'll go along with it. At the time, I was hustling or the thing couldn't have happened."

# What Do Tennis Terms "Seeding," "Love," "Let," "Break," "Deuce," and "Fault" Mean?

"**S**eeding" is derived from sowing seeds into a selected environment which will yield desirable results. **Webster's Sports Dictionary** defines "seed" as "(1) To schedule tournament players or teams so that superior ones will not meet in early rounds. (2) To rank tournament players or teams on the basis of their demonstrated or estimated abilities."

Seeding can apply to any sport, but it has a long tradition in tennis. Bud Collins's **Modern Encyclopedia of Tennis** states that seeding was first used at Wimbledon in 1924 and adopted by Forest Hills for the 1927 U.S. Open.

Seedings are based on past performance. Standings, won-lost records, and computer analysis determine the seeds.

"Love" is the tennis term meaning zero. It probably derived centuries ago from the French word **l'oeuf,** for "the egg," referring to a goose egg— a zero.

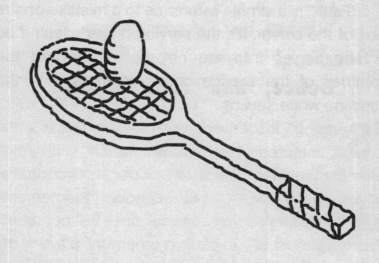

The term "let" comes from the Anglo-Saxon word **lettan,** meaning "to hinder." If a serve lands in the service box, having been hindered by hitting the top of the net, a let is called and the serve is replayed.

One player "breaks" another by winning the other's service game. The term probably was applied because loss of service harms, and can even break, one's chances of winning the set. A service loss can break a player's spirits as well.

"Deuce" is slang for the numeral 2 and a derivative of the French **deux.** When a game is at deuce (tied at 40–40), one player must score two successive points to win.

"Fault" is a simple reference to a mistake on the part of the server. It's the serving player's fault if he or she serves into the net, serves beyond the confines of the service court, or steps onto the baseline while serving.

# Who Hit the Longest Home Run?

The longest home run on record was a 565-foot clout hit at old Griffith Stadium on April 17, 1953. Mickey Mantle, a switch-hitter for the New York Yankees, was batting righthanded against lefthanded pitcher Chuck Stobbs of the Washington Senators. Mantle hit a rising line drive that nicked the lower righthand corner of a huge beer sign atop a football scoreboard behind the left-centerfield bleachers. The ball left the stadium, carried across a street, and landed in the back yard of a home.

This blow was responsible for the expression "tape-measure home run" because the Yankees' publicity director, Red Patterson, immediately left the press box, found himself a tape measure and paced off the distance to the spot where witnesses said the ball came down.

Mantle—and perhaps others—probably have hit longer home runs. That's certainly the view of Stobbs, 69, who lives in retirement in Sarasota, Florida.

"He hit 'em pretty far against a lot of people," Chuck says. "The only reason they remember this one is because they marked the spot on the beer sign where the ball left the park, but Bucky Harris (the Senators' manager) later made them take the marker down.

"I got Mantle out pretty good later on. I think he was 2 for 25 off me one year, but nobody ever talks about that."

## Did a Jockey Come Back from the Dead?

Horse racing jockey Ralph Neves rode 3,771 winners during a 30-year riding career that lasted from 1934 to 1964. He was elected to the Hall of Fame in 1960. Not bad for a man who died on the track in 1936 (only to recover and ride the next day).

The bizarre incident occurred on May 12, 1936, at Bay Meadows race track in San Mateo, California. During a race, Ralph was tossed off his horse. He lay on the ground unconscious, and was taken to a nearby hospital where he was pronounced dead and sent to the morgue.

"I was supposed to meet a doctor friend of mine for dinner," said Ralph, recalling his near-death experience, which he laughed about for years afterward. "He asked at the track why I was taken off my mounts for the rest of the day and they told him I was at the hospital. They told him I was dead."

Fortunately for Ralph, his doctor friend raced to the hospital. "Apparently, he found some signs of life and gave me an injection of adrenalin into my heart. Then I woke up."

Ralph, who had been unconscious for over two hours, bolted out of the morgue wearing only his riding pants and one boot (the other was taken off to put a toe tag on the "corpse"). He hailed a taxi cab and was driven to Bay Meadows track.

When Ralph reported back to work, he was told to sit out the rest of the day. But he was back in the saddle again the following afternoon, having missed just half a day because of his "death."

# Why Don't Relief Pitchers Use Golf Carts Anymore?

Like doubleheaders, bullpen carts have pretty much disappeared from the game, and that's a shame because they were a true slice of Americana.

It was fun to see a reliever, called on to save the day, ride into action in a golf cart topped by a ridiculous, oversized baseball cap. But the bullpens in today's cookie-cutter stadiums are located along the foul lines, a short walk from the pitching mound. In the older parks where the pens are situated beyond the outfield fences, the pitchers have gotten used to jogging to their jobs.

The history of bullpen carts can be traced to 1951 when Hank Greenberg, then general manager of the Cleveland Indians, thought it would be a great publicity stunt to have pitchers brought in on golf carts. Yankee manager Casey Stengel objected, saying, "Yankee pitchers don't ride in golf carts, they ride in Cadillacs."

The next night Greenberg had a Cadillac in the bullpen for the Yankees, but New York's Allie Reynolds spoiled the joke by throwing not just a complete game but a no-hitter. The automobile wasn't needed and was gone the next day.

# Who Started the Gatorade Dump?

Former New York Giants linebacker Harry Carson and defensive lineman Jim Burt started the tradition of dumping Gatorade on coaches. The first wet victory celebration took place in 1985, after a 17–3 victory over the Washington Redskins at Giants Stadium, when Harry and Jim sneaked up on Coach Bill Parcells and showered him.

"It was really Jim's idea," said Harry. "But I helped pull it off on Parcells the first time."

Like most athletes, Harry was superstitious. For good luck, he drenched Coach Parcells several more times after victories that season and after each win during the 1986 season. The 1986 drenchings were a real good luck charm. That season, the Giants won 17 of their 19 games, including the Super Bowl.

What did it feel like to be drenched from head to toe with Gatorade? "Cold!" says Coach Parcells. "But it felt good, too, because it meant we had won."

## What Do the Letters "C" and "A" on Hockey Uniforms Mean?

The "C" and "A" have been used on hockey uniforms since the 1940s to designate captains and alternate captains. The jobs are not merely honorary. Captains and alternates are the only players who are supposed to communicate with the referee and linesmen and serve as the liaisons between the bench and players on the ice.

Captains are chosen by their teammates or coaches, and the selection can be thorny. There was an uproar in Hartford during the 1990–91 season when Ron Francis was stripped of his C by the Whalers' coaching staff, a signal that preceded his trade to Pittsburgh.

In 1989, Toronto management took away Brad Marsh's A and gave it to Gary Leeman. But Leeman refused, and Marsh wouldn't take it back.

There have also been some shining moments. When Wayne Gretzky joined the Los Angeles Kings, Dave Taylor volunteered to give the Great One his captaincy. Taylor thought the C would mean more to the officials if Gretzky wore it.

Perhaps the North Stars in 1990–91 exemplified the true meaning of the honor. Basil McRae and Brian Bellows shared the C—a symbol of the teamwork that led Minnesota to the Stanley Cup finals. "No one guy can be the captain of his team," McRae said. "It's a 20-man effort out there every night."

# Why Is Home-Court Advantage
# So Important in the NBA?

In the sport of basketball, all courts station the baskets 10 feet high, and the dimensions of the court are exactly the same wherever a game is played. Why then does playing on your home court mean so much?

The home-court advantage was just that during the 1996–97 NBA regular season (home teams won 684 of 1,189 games for a winning percentage of 58 percent), and it obviously was important during the playoffs (home teams won 48 of 72 games for a winning percentage of 67 percent).

What explains this? Well, several advantages are provided by the home court. There's the "home cookin' theory" (players are more relaxed when they literally go home after the game). There's the "loud crowd factor" which may influence the referees.

And there's the visiting team "jet-lag syndrome" (players don't have time to recover from a long flight, much less prepare for the game or practice on an enemy court with its unfamiliar shooting background). One favorite is the "power of positive thinking philosophy" (players on their home court think they have an advantage, therefore they perform better).

However, none of these factors is peculiar to the NBA. Road teams in other sports face the same problems, yet no other professional sports league can come close to matching the NBA in road futility.

The real reason it's so difficult to win on the road in the NBA is the league's scheduling. It's not unusual for an NBA team to play three games in five nights in three different cities. "You don't find schedules like that in other sports," says Tom Heinsohn, a former player and coach for the Boston Celtics who now broadcasts their games. "In football, you play one game a week, and in baseball, teams usually play three games in a city at a time."

The only sports league that can match the travel of the 82-game NBA season is the National Hockey League, which also plays 82 games. But the NHL schedule goes easier on road teams. Teams rarely play back-to-back games in different cities.

Perhaps not having a national network television contract forces the NHL to be more budget-conscious, which would result in a less rigorous schedule. NHL divisions are set up geographically, so as many games as possible are close to home.

Hockey teams usually make one long trip to take care of road games with distant divisions. For example, when an NHL team from the Western Conference travels East, it usually plays the New York Rangers and Islanders, the New Jersey Devils, and the Philadelphia Flyers in successive games.

In the NBA, the divisions are also aligned geographically, but not as strictly. Atlanta plays in the

Central Division, but must travel often and far to play division rivals Chicago, Milwaukee, and Detroit.

## Who Invented Water Skiing?

Water skiing was invented on June 29, 1922, when an 18-year-old named Ralph Samuelson glided briefly across the surface of Lake Pepin in Minnesota, 60 miles southeast of Minneapolis, on a pair of 8-foot-long, 9-inch-wide planks he bought at a local lumberyard.

Samuelson, who lived in nearby Lake City, softened one end of each ski in his mother's wash boiler and curved up the ends by clamping them in vises. He fastened a leather strap in the middle of each ski to hold his feet in place and bought 100 feet of sash cord to use as a tow rope.

Apparently a showman as well as a sportsman, Samuelson was paid for his derring-do and in 1925 also became the first water ski jumper. That summer, during an exhibition, the wake from a passing boat stripped one of the skis from his feet. He was able to finish on the other ski and incorporated it into his routine; thus was slalom water skiing born.

For years, Fred Waller, inventor of the film process known as Cinerama, was incorrectly credited with having created water skiing. Waller, however, first skied on Long Island Sound in 1924, two years after Samuelson cavorted on Lake Pepin.

## Who Pitched the Most Frustrating No-Hitter?

The first pitcher to throw a complete game no-hitter and lose was Ken Johnson of the Houston Colt .45s (later the Astros) in 1964. He lost to the Reds 1–0, when, in the top of the ninth inning, he committed a three-base throwing error on Pete Rose's bunt and Nellie Fox booted a grounder, allowing Rose to score.

Hard luck was nothing new for Johnson, a righthander whose lifetime record for seven teams was 91–106. "One game against the Phillies, they had a 'Runs For Johnson Night,' and any woman with a run in her stockings got in for free," he recalled of his Colt .45 days. "And then Jim Bunning beat us with a one-hitter."

Steve Barber and Stu Miller of the Baltimore Orioles combined to pitch a no-hitter and yet lost to the Detroit Tigers in 1967. Andy Hawkins of the New York Yankees allowed no hits against the Chicago White Sox in 1990 but lost the game after four runs scored on three errors and two walks in the bottom of the eighth inning.

Since the White Sox won when they set down the Yankees in the top of the ninth, Hawkins had no opportunity to pitch nine innings. Therefore, his no-hitter was erased from the record books on September 4, 1991, when baseball's Committee for Statistical Accuracy defined a no-hitter as a complete hitless game of nine innings or more.

The new ruling was quickly enforced when Matt Young of the Red Sox no-hit the Cleveland Indians in April 1992. But the Boston lefty walked seven batters and lost 2–1. Because Cleveland won the game, they didn't have to bat in the bottom of the ninth, and Matt was denied his official no-hitter.

"A no-hitter is supposed to be where you strike out the last guy and the catcher comes out and jumps in your arms. A loss is a loss," said Matt.

## Who Is the Most Daring Race Car Driver?

Automobile racing is exciting but dangerous. It tests the performance of both the car and the driver. During an IndyCar race, the driver's heart rate can accelerate to 195 beats per minute—that's faster than an astronaut's heart rate at blast-off!

The 1985 Indianapolis 500 is remembered for the wild ride Danny Sullivan took on his way to the checkered flag. Danny was driving in second place behind the leader, Mario Andretti. Going into the first turn of lap 120 (there are 200 laps), Danny decided to make his move. He veered inside of Mario's car at 200 miles per hour. It was a dangerous move, especially with 80 laps still to go. "I thought there were just 12 laps left. I'd read the pit board wrong," said Danny.

While Danny was trying to pass Mario, the two cars touched and Danny almost lost control. Danny's car started smoking and he had to hold on during a 360-degree spin. "I thought that was all she wrote, but when the smoke cleared, I was straight again," said Danny.

Miraculously, he drove through it and later, on the 140th lap, Danny passed Mario at the same point, down the front straight and into the first turn as before. This time he got it right and went on to win the race by 2.5 seconds. "I knew I had a few more laps this time, and I didn't want to screw it up again," Danny said.

# Who Were the Steagles?

In 1943, the call for able-bodied men to serve in World War II depleted the rosters of the Philadelphia Eagles and the Pittsburgh Steelers, and on June 19 the league granted permission for the teams to merge for one season.

Though the official name was Phil-Pitt Eagles, the team was called the "Steagles." They were jointly coached by the Steelers' Walt Kiesling and the Eagles' Earle "Greasy" Neale, who made the best of the situation by finishing 5–4–1, third in the Eastern Division and one game out of first place.

The team consisted mainly of free agents and rookies, though former Eagle end Bill Hewitt came out of retirement to play, wearing a helmet for the first time (helmets had not been required when Hewitt had played previously). Leroy Zimmerman was the quarterback, with 20-year-old Allie Sherman backing him up. The Steagles preferred to stay on the ground, and Jack Hinkle finished second in the league in rushing with 571 yards on 116 carries. The Steagles had two home fields, playing four games in Shibe Park in Philadelphia and two at Forbes Field in Pittsburgh.

The two-team combination vanished at the end of the season, but the Steelers, still troubled by financial and roster problems, merged with the Chicago Cardinals for 1944 under the name Card-Pitt. The name was an unfortunate choice. As the team bumbled to an 0–10 record, it became known as the "Carpets."

## Who Invented the Go-Kart?

The first go-kart was made in 1956 by Art Ingles, a professional race car designer from southern California. Art knew how to make fast big cars—he helped build cars that raced in the Indy 500 during the 1950s—but Art also wanted to make fast little cars.

Art's first go-kart was made with a lawn mower engine and a frame of metal tubing. Sitting with his knees bent so they almost touched his chin, Art sped around the parking lot of Pasadena's Rose Bowl at 30 miles per hour! Crowds gathered in amazement, and the karting phenomenon was born.

# Which College Football Program Has the Worst Record?

The first Division I-A or I-AA school in the nation to lose 500 games is Kansas State. After 102 years of playing the game (or rather, **trying** to play it), the Wildcats' record is 366 wins, 548 losses and 40 ties. No school has lost as many football games as Kansas State.

For the period from 1946 to 1991 (the most current year statistics are available), KSU ranks last in the nation in scoring offense and last in scoring defense, and since 1954 the old Purple and White also have been last in total offense. From 1936 through 1992 the Wildcats (or should it be Pussycats?) have had only four winning seasons.

Happily for Kansas State fans, the 60-year curve seems to be headed up as KSU has now enjoyed five consecutive winning seasons. In 1997, the Wildcats finished the season with a brilliant record of 11–1 and a Fiesta Bowl victory.

Bill Snyder, architect of the encouraging turnaround, is KSU's 32nd head coach. State may not bring any Big 12 championships home to Manhattan, Kansas, soon—Nebraska has a lock on the conference title—so Snyder will need to keep his bizarre sense of humor. "A loss is not the end of the world," he told his team upon his arrival in 1989. "If it was, you guys would have been pushing up daisies with your toes a long time ago."

## Who Created the Box Score?

Henry Chadwick compiled the first box score for baseball, published in the **New York Clipper** in the summer of 1859. The game was played between two Brooklyn, New York, teams—the Stars and the Excelsiors. The Stars won 17–12, scoring ten runs in the top of the ninth inning.

The make-up of Chadwick's original box score—so called for the old newspaper custom of placing the data in a boxed-off section on the page—consisted of five columns devoted to each player's runs, hits, putouts, assists, and errors. Also included was a line score, the umpire, and time of game.

Chadwick's box score creation did not appear regularly in newspapers until the organization of the National League in 1876. As the game's popularity grew, the box score became an integral device for reporting data comprehensively in a condensed space.

Known as "the Father of Baseball," Chadwick was the game's first writer and historian. He published the original rule book in 1859 and served as chairman of the first Rules Committee. Born in England, Chadwick relied on his cricket background to promote baseball in America and was considered the most knowledgeable source of the day.

# What Is Meant by a "Rubber Game"?

You often hear sportscasters call the third and deciding game of a baseball series the "rubber game." The term is traced back to 16th-century English sports by the **Oxford English Dictionary.**

"Rubber" is defined by **Webster's Sports Dictionary** as "A three-game match or series; a series or match in which one side must win two out of three games...used attributively in the United States to refer to a final game or match played between two individuals or teams that have previously split an even number of games or matches."

The word was originally used in the English sport of bowls, and a rubber in bridge is two games taken by one team. A "rubber game" today usually refers to the final and deciding game in a best-of-three or best-of-five series. But the seventh game of a World Series could be called a "rubber game," too.

# Who Started the Two-Minute Warning in Football?

The two-minute warning is an unwritten rule in the NFL, and such traditions die hard.

Until 1970, the official time was kept by the line judge, and it frequently differed from the time on the scoreboard clock. The league started notifying coaches at the two-minute mark initially as a courtesy, to let them know the exact time. The break allowed the scoreboard and official clocks to be synchronized and also gave the coaches a chance to plan strategy.

Today, the scoreboard clock is official and the coaches know exactly how much time is left, but the NFL still takes a break for the warning. One reason is that the timeout (which actually lasts 1 minute, 50 seconds) still allows the coaches to discuss strategy and inform the officials when they might call their remaining timeouts.

Another reason probably is television. Each break gives the networks a chance to squeeze in three more 30-second commercial spots during what often is an exciting part of the game when more viewers are likely to be watching.

# Who Invented the Snowboard?

**S**nowboarding is a relatively new sport that has roots in skiing, surfing, and skateboarding. Exactly who dreamed up snowboarding is unclear. The truth is, no one person did.

The sport of snowboarding started out with a toy called the "Snurfer," which was a snow toy similar to a water ski with a rope on the front end. The Snurfer was invented in the 1960s by Sherman Poppen. One day Sherman was outside sledding with his children when his daughter stood up on her sled. This inspired Sherman to build the Snurfer, which was sold by the Brunswick Sporting Goods Company. "The Snurfer will become the Hula-Hoop of wintertime," said Sherman.

In the 1970s, a man named Jake Burton, who had been given a Snurfer when he was a kid, invented a better snowboard by making his Snurfer wider and adding two skegs (fins) on the bottom. Jake's board also had a rubber water ski binding for the front foot. The bindings were a major breakthrough and really marked the first difference between a Snurfer and a snowboard.

The bindings kept the front foot firmly in place, and riders soon discovered an increase in control and maneuverability. Since Jake's boards were stronger and lighter, carving turns in the snow at 55 miles per hour became easier and the action more stable. By the late 1970s, snowboarding had taken off.

By the late 1980s, more and more "rad dudes" were bringing their snowboards to ski areas. Soon, professional competitions were being held around the world. At the 1998 Nagano Winter Olympics, snowboarding debuted as a medal sport. Is there no stopping it? According to a 1993 poll, if snowboarding continues to grow at its current rate, it will be more popular than skiing by the year 2012!

# What Is the Most Embarrassing Moment in Baseball History?

During his major league baseball career as a utility infielder, Steve Lyons didn't play much. But when he did, you knew it by his dirt-encrusted, grass-stained uniform.

In a 1990 game against Detroit, Steve was making a rare start at first base for the Chicago White Sox. At bat, he attempted to hit safely by dragging a bunt. The ball trickled perfectly between the pitcher's mound and first base. Realizing that the play would be close, Steve dived headlong into first, creating a massive dirt cloud.

"Safe!" barked the umpire, setting off an argument with Tiger players. While the dust cleared, Steve was feeling uncomfortable because dirt was falling down the inside of his uniform bottoms. So he matter-of-factly pulled his pants down and brushed off the dirt. Steve soon realized he had dropped his drawers on national television! He immediately hitched up his britches, suitably embarrassed.

Some teammates wondered if Steve, who is known as "Psycho" for his down-and-dirty attitude, hadn't pulled an intentional prank. "I may be off the wall, but I'm not stupid," he insisted.

Luckily, Steve heeded his mother's advice and, at the time, was wearing clean shorts under his uniform pants. "She's the one who always told me to wear clean underwear in case something happened and I had to show them to strangers."

## Which City Has the Best Winning Percentage?

The honor of being the nation's number 1 sports city goes to either New York or Boston, depending on the system of selection one uses.

If we consider the number of titles won in the four major sports—World Series, NFL championships or Super Bowls, NBA titles, and Stanley Cup championships—New York wins easily. Big Apple teams have won 46 titles (30 in baseball, 8 in hockey, 6 in football, 2 in basketball). Boston has won 27 (6 in baseball, 5 in hockey, 16 in basketball). Chicago finishes third with 19 championships and Los Angeles is fourth with 13.

We think this system is skewed, though. It doesn't compensate for the fact that New York had three teams in baseball and two teams in football for much of the century, whereas Boston has had only one team in baseball since 1953 and didn't have a pro football team until 1960.

A better method is to take these four cities and then determine their winning percentage in those championship games or series in which they were involved. Since AFL championships also contributed to the "winning" image of a particular city, we're going to take those into account as well.

By this manner of reckoning, the winner is—envelope please—**Boston.** Boston teams have won 52.9 percent of those championships they have contested (27 of 51). New York has won 50.5 percent (46 of 91), Chicago 45.2 percent (19 of 42), and Los Angeles 37.1 percent (13 of 35). Long live the Beantowners!